How to Raise and Train a
GERMAN SHORTHAIRED POINTER

By ARTHUR LIEBERS

Distributed in the U.S.A. by T.F.H. Publications, Inc., 211 West Sylvania Avenue, P.O. Box 27, Neptune City, N.J. 07753; in England by T.F.H. (Gt. Britain) Ltd., 13 Nutley Lane, Reigate, Surrey; in Canada by Clarke, Irwin & Company, Clarwin House, 791 St. Clair Avenue West, Toronto 10, Ontario; in Southeast Asia by Y. W. Ong, 9 Lorong 36 Geylang, Singapore 14; in Australia and the south Pacific by Pet Imports Pty. Ltd., P.O. Box 149, Brookvale 2100, N.S.W., Australia.
Published by T.F.H. Publications, Inc. Ltd., The British Crown Colony of Hong Kong.

Photography by Louise Van der Meid with the
cooperation of Mr. & Mrs. Walt Shellenbarger
of Gretchenhof Kennels, Paul & Shirley McComack
of Callmac Kennels, Bill Hicks, Marvin & Greta
Hinch, Robert & Ivy Laufman, Harvey Warholm,
and Richard Golden and daughter.
  The models are Heidi Shellenbarger, Michael
and Deborah McComack.

ISBN 0-87666-301-3

Contents

German Shorthaired Pointers are attractive, medium-sized dogs developed in Germany during the 19th century. Your Shorthair will be a friendly, reliable pet as well as a useful hunter. He is easy to train and has a calm, steady disposition.

1. History of the Breed

The German Shorthaired Pointer is a breed that was actually "made to order" by experienced German breeders. After many efforts, they successfully combined the characteristics of an excellent hunter with those of an ideal house pet. The dog has extremely keen scenting powers, a high degree of canine intelligence and a friendly, non-aggressive disposition.

Like the better-known Weimaraner, the German Shorthaired Pointer is truly an all-purpose sporting dog. He matures fairly early—puppies only six months old have been known to do creditable jobs of pointing after very little training —and is equally well suited for hunting furred or feathered game. Most trainers recommend breaking him in on birds, and he has shown himself to be particularly helpful in hunting quail, pheasant, grouse, partridge, woodcock and duck, for example. He is also very good for other kinds of game, such as deer, rabbits, coon and possum.

In addition to his primary role as a pointer, you can readily train the dog to retrieve on land or from the water. His thick, water-resilient coat and his webbed feet make him a well-equipped all-weather retriever.

In spite of all these advantages, the German Shorthaired Pointer is not one of the more popular sporting breeds. Probably this is so because he is a relatively slow-moving dog, often unable to compete with the flashier, faster pointers and setters in open field competition. His sturdy, bulky body was not designed for speed. He is particularly careful, however, picking up even the faintest scent and following it to the game. Usually he works with his head held low, due to the hound in his background.

For the man who is more interested in a pleasant day's hunting than in winning field trophies, the German Shorthaired Pointer is ideal. He covers a limited range in a thorough, leisurely manner, and can switch from water-fowling to upland game hunting.

Many qualities make the German Shorthaired Pointer a wonderful house pet. Unlike many of the more highly-strung sporting dogs, this breed is notably tractable and easy to train. The dog seems anxious to learn and to do what you ask of him. Puppies are unusually easy to housebreak, and an adult dog is almost always cooperative.

Although the dog shows some reserve toward strangers, he is seldom hostile, and seems to prefer making the first advances himself rather than accepting them from humans. You can train him to be an excellent watchdog.

The breed is sturdy enough to put up with the abuse a house pet takes from small children, and the average German Shorthaired Pointer is extremely patient with them.

The dog's size is another good feature. Males are generally about 55 to

70 pounds; females about 10 pounds lighter. In height, males are about 23 to 25 inches, while females are 21 to 23 inches. A dog of this size does not take up too much room in a small house or apartment or on the seat of an automobile if you travel. Because of this, German Shorthairs can live in small quarters, as long as they are exercised regularly (see page 26).

Unlike other pointers, the dog's tail is ordinarily docked to about one-third its normal length. This eliminates the danger of a swinging tail doing unintentional damage to household objects. (The main reason for docking the tail is to prevent injury to it as the dog ranges through brush and trees while hunting.) Also, because of his short coat, he sheds very little.

THE GERMAN SHORTHAIRED POINTER'S BACKGROUND

The German Shorthaired Pointer was first developed as a breed in the 17th century, when hunting was still an important source of food in Europe. At that time German breeders imported several Spanish Pointers. These dogs were of predominately hound blood, although they were used as pointers. To increase the versatility of the Spanish Pointer, the breeders crossed the dog with the old German Bloodhound. The result was a bulky, houndlike dog that became known as the German Pointer. He could not only point birds and rabbits, but also trail larger game. It is interesting to note that this breed became popular with poachers, who slipped into baronial estates and game preserves for sessions of night hunting.

Toward the middle 1800's, the Germans became dissatisfied with the bulkiness of the German Pointer. Besides, it appeared that the breed had lost some of its original scenting ability. Therefore, the breeders began a concerted breeding program, aiming for what was finally achieved in the modern German Shorthaired Pointer.

To make the breed slimmer, they brought in some good strains of American and English Pointers and began a series of selective crossbreedings. From these infusions the breed gained speed and its scenting powers were improved. Another advantage was the reinforcement of the dog's instincts for trailing and retrieving.

It wasn't long before the new breed was producing litters that were true to type and, in 1872, a German Shorthaired Pointer was registered in the German Kennel Club Stud Book. The German parent organization of the breed set up physical standards as well as standards of performance in the field, and the strain improved both in ability and appearance.

In the following years the new breed became quite well known in most European countries. Although they were never very popular in England, the "Shorthairs" became more and more prominent on the Continent. Beginning in the early 1900's, German Shorthaired Pointers from many European countries competed in world-wide shows for the title of "World Seiger" or champion.

In the United States the breed was still almost unknown, although there may have been one or two of the dogs in the west, probably brought in by German immigrants, and perhaps a few among the German families in the Hudson River Valley region of New York State. The first formal notice of German

Although your Shorthair may lack the flash and daring of a Setter, he is extraordinarily sharp-scented and follows the "sniff" of game persistently to its source. He is just as effective at waterfowling as at tracking down upland game.

Shorthaired Pointers came around 1925, when a Dr. Charles Thornton of Montana set up a kennel and began breeding them. In 1930, the American Kennel Club gave recognition to the breed. Acceptance of the dogs has been slow, but they are now among the fifty most popular breeds in AKC recognition, and a substantial number of them are registered each year with the Field Dog Stud Book, which registers sporting dog breeds.

STANDARDS OF THE BREED

The standards which have been adopted by the German Shorthaired Pointer Club of America and approved by the American Kennel Club set the present-day ideal for which breeders are aiming. It is by these standards that the dog is judged in the show ring. However, even the most perfect specimen falls short of the standards in some respect. It's also impossible, even for a breeder or veterinarian, to tell how a puppy will shape up as an adult dog. The chances are that he will inherit those qualities for which his father and mother—or sire and dam in dog language—were bred, and if both his parents and grandparents had good show records, he may have excellent possibilities.

Here, then, are the standards.

GENERAL APPEARANCE: The over-all picture which is created in the observer's eye should be that of an aristocratic, well-balanced, symmetrical animal with conformation indicating power, endurance and agility and a look of intelligence and animation. The dog should be neither unduly small nor conspicuously large. It should rather give the impression of medium size, but be like the proper hunter, "with a short back, but standing over plenty of ground." Tall, leggy individuals seldom possess endurance or sound movement.

Dogs which are ponderous or unbalanced because of excess substance should be definitely rejected. The first impression should be that of a keenness which denotes full enthusiasm for work without indication of nervous or flighty character. Movement should be alertly co-ordinated without waste motion. Grace of outline, clean-cut head, sloping shoulders, deep breast, powerful back, strong quarters, good bone composition, adequate muscle, well-carried tail and taut coat, all of which should combine to produce a look of nobility and an indication of anatomical structure essential to correct gait which must indicate a heritage of purposefully conducted breeding.

HEAD: Clean-cut, neither too light nor too heavy, in proper proportion to the body. Skull should be reasonably broad, arched on side and slightly round on top. Scissura (median line between the eyes at the forehead) not too deep, occipital bone not as conspicuous as in the case of the Pointer. The foreface should rise gradually from nose to forehead—not resembling the Roman nose. This is more strongly pronounced in the male than in the female, as befitting his sex. The chops should fall away from the somewhat projecting nose. Lips should be full and deep, never flewy. The chops should not fall over too much, but form a proper fold in the angle. The jaw should be powerful and the muscles well developed. The line to the forehead should rise gradually and should never possess a definite stop as in the case of the Pointer, but rather a stop-effect when viewed from the side, due to the position of the eyebrows. The muzzle should be sufficiently long to enable the dog to seize properly and to facilitate his carrying game a long time. A pointed muzzle is not desirable. The entire head should never give the impression of tapering to a point. The depth should be in the right proportion to the length, both in the muzzle and in the skull proper.

EARS: Ears should be broad and set fairly high, lie flat and never hang away from the head. Placement should be above eye level. The ears, when laid in front without being pulled, should about meet the lip angle. In the case of heavier dogs, they should be correspondingly longer.

EYES: The eyes should be of medium size, full of intelligence and expressive, good-humored, and yet radiating energy, neither protruding nor sunk. The eyelids should close well. The best color is a dark shade of brown. Light yellow, china or wall (bird of prey) eyes are not desirable.

NOSE: Brown, the larger the better, nostrils well opened and broad. Flesh-colored and spotted noses are not desirable.

TEETH: The teeth should be strong and healthy. The molars should intermesh properly. Incisors should fit close in a true scissor bite. Jaws should be neither overshot nor undershot.

NECK: Of adequate length to permit the jaws reaching game to be retrieved, sloping downwards on beautifully curving lines. The nape should be rather muscular, becoming gradually larger towards the shoulders. Moderate hound-like throatiness permitted.

BREAST AND THORAX: The breast in general should give the impression of depth rather than breadth, for all that, it should be in correct proportion to the other parts of the body with fair depth of chest. The ribs forming the thorax

"Will somebody please get me out of here?" Naturally, he doesn't enjoy being locked in; nevertheless, your Shorthair will be as patient as this one if it becomes necessary to keep him confined so he can travel or for some other purpose. Notice, too, the shape of his ears. Broad and flat, they hang quite close to his head.

should be well-curved and not flat; they should not be absolutely round or barrel-shaped. Ribs that are entirely round prevent the necessary expansion of the chest when taking breath. The back ribs should reach well down. The circumference of the breast immediately behind the elbows should be smaller than that of the breast about a hands-breadth behind elbows, so that the upper arm has room for movement.

BACK AND LOINS: Back should be short, strong and straight with slight rise from root of tail to withers. Excessively long or hog-backed should be penalized. Loin strong, of moderate length and slightly arched. Tuck-up should be apparent.

ASSEMBLY OF BACK MEMBERS: The hips should be broad with hip sockets wide apart and fall slightly toward the tail in a graceful curve. Thighs strong and well muscled. Stifles well bent. Hock joints should be well angulated with strong, straight bone structure from hock to pad. Angulation of both stifle and hock joints should be such as to combine maximum combination of both drive and traction. Hocks should turn neither in nor out.

9

ASSEMBLY OF FRONT MEMBERS: The shoulders should be sloping, movable, well covered with muscle. The shoulder blades should lie flat. The upper arm (also called the cross bar, *i.e.* the bones between the shoulder and elbow joints) should be as long as possible, standing away somewhat from the trunk so that the straight and closely muscled legs, when viewed from in front, should appear to be parallel. Elbows which stand away from the body or are pressed right into same indicate toes turning inwards or outwards, which should be regarded as faults. Pasterns should be strong, short and nearly vertical.

FEET: Should be compact, close-knit and round to spoon-shaped. The toes sufficiently arched and heavily nailed. The pad should be strong and hard.

COAT AND SKIN: The skin should look close and tight. The hair should be short and thick and feel tough and hard to the hand; it is somewhat longer on the underside of the tail and the back edge of the haunches. It is softer, thinner and shorter on the ears and the head.

TAIL: Is set high and firm, and must be docked, leaving approximately two-fifths of length. The tail hangs down when the dog is quiet, is held horizontally when he is walking, never turned over the back or considerably bent but violently wagged when he is on the search.

BONES: Thin and fine bones are by no means desirable in a dog which should be able to work over any and every country and should possess strength. The main importance accordingly is laid not so much on the size as being in proper proportion to the body. Dogs with coarse bones are handicapped in agility of movement and speed.

DESIRABLE WEIGHT AND HEIGHT: Males—55 to 70 pounds. Females —45 to 60 pounds. Males—23 to 25 inches. Females—21 to 23 inches at the shoulders.

COLOR: Solid liver, liver and white spotted, liver and white spotted and ticked, liver and white ticked, liver roan. Any colors other than liver and white (gray white) are not permitted.

Symmetry and field quality are most essential. A dog well balanced in all points is preferable to one with outstanding good qualities and defects. A smooth, lithe gait is most desirable.

FAULTS: Bone structure too clumsy or too light, head too large, too many wrinkles in forehead, dish-faced, snipy muzzle, ears too long, pointy or fleshy, flesh-coloured nose, eyes too light, too round or too closely set together, excessive throatiness, cowhocks, feet or elbows turned inward or outward, down on pasterns, loose shoulders, sway-back, black coat or tri-colored, any colors except liver or some combination of liver and white.

2. Selecting Your Dog

How much you spend for your Shorthair should depend on the purpose for which you are buying him. If you are planning to show your dog, then you want a puppy with good bloodlines and the possibility of developing into a champion. This may cost several hundred dollars, and if you are not an expert on dogs, you should have an expert help you make your selection.

If you want your Shorthair to be solely a pet or companion or guard for children, you can acquire a good one for considerably less money. The fact that his conformation may be a bit off and his ancestors weren't champions won't make him any less valuable for your purposes.

WHERE TO BUY YOUR DOG

If it is a show dog you're seeking, you'll probably do best by getting your puppy from a kennel that specializes in this breed or a private breeder who exhibits. If you have the chance to visit a dog show, the experienced exhibitors there may have puppies for sale or can direct you to a good source.

If you're not so concerned about bloodlines, you may be able to find the right Shorthair for you at a pet shop or the pet section of a department store. If you live far from any source, you can buy a good one by mail. Several of the larger mail order houses are in the dog business, too, and most kennels will ship a dog to you with the guarantee that the puppy is purebred and healthy.

THE PUPPY'S PAPERS

If you are investing in a purebred dog, obtain the necessary papers from the seller, especially if you are planning to show or breed your dog. Usually the litter will have been registered with the American Kennel Club. This is necessary before the individual puppy can be registered. The breeder should provide you with an Application for Registration signed by the owner of the puppy's mother. Then you select a name for your dog (it must be 25 letters or less, and cannot duplicate the name of another dog of the breed, or be the name of a living person without his written permission). Enter the selected name on the form, fill in the blanks that make you the owner of record, and send it to the American Kennel Club, 221 Park Avenue South, New York, N.Y., with the required fee. In a few weeks if all is in order you will receive the blue and white Certificate of Registration with your dog's stud book number.

Some owners of German Shorthaired Pointers prefer to register them with the Field Dog Stud Book, 222 West Adams Street, Chicago 6, Illinois, which registers pointers and setters and almost all field trial bird dogs. This organization provides you with pedigree papers and certificates of registration.

Looking as though they all need a home, these pups peer wistfully over the edge of their box. You'll have a hard time choosing which little fellow to take. But remember no matter how lovable the pup—you should have his health checked by a vet before you close the deal.

THE PEDIGREE

The pedigree of your dog is a tracing of his family tree. Often the breeder will have the pedigree of the dog's dam and sire and may make out a copy for you. Or you can write to the American Kennel Club once your dog has been registered and ask for a pedigree. The fee depends on how many generations back you want the pedigree traced. In addition to giving the immediate ancestors of your dog, the pedigree will show whether there are any champions or dogs that have won obedience degrees in his lineage. If you are planning selective breeding, the pedigree is also helpful to enable you to find other German Shorthaired Pointers that have the same general family background.

A HEALTHY PUPPY

The healthy puppy will be active, gay and alert, with bright, shiny eyes. He should not have running eyes or nose. If the puppy in which you are interested seems listless, it may be that he has just eaten and wants to sleep for a while. Come back for a second look in a few hours, to see if he is more active.

In buying a puppy—especially a higher-priced one—it is always wise to make your purchase subject to the approval of a veterinarian. The seller will usually allow you 8 hours in which to take the puppy to a vet to have his health checked. However, come to a clear agreement on what happens if the vet rejects the puppy. It should be understood whether rejection means that you can get your money back or merely choice of another puppy from the same litter.

Usually, in buying a puppy, you will have a choice among several in a litter, or even better, among several litters. It is advisable to have someone with you who knows the breed. If this is not possible, before you select a dog reread the standards on pages 7-10 to give you an idea of the desirable and undesirable features of the breed.

If you are following the usual procedure, you will be acquiring a puppy about 6 or 8 weeks old. You will probably do best if you settle for a medium-sized puppy, with straight legs and a medium-sized back. At that age it is still too early to be able to tell much about how the puppy will shape up as a grown dog. If you are planning to use the dog as a hunter, try to get one whose parents have hunted. It is often possible to see the dam when you are examining a litter with a view to buying, and her behaviour and disposition should give an indication of what she contributed to the puppies.

MALE OR FEMALE?

Unless you want to breed your pet and raise a litter of puppies it doesn't matter whether you choose a male or female. Both sexes are pretty much the same in disposition and character, and both make equally good pets. The male may be a bit more inclined to roam; the female is more of a homebody. A female's daily walks needn't be as long as the male's.

If you choose a female but decide you don't want to raise puppies, your dog can be spayed and will remain a healthy, lively pet.

ADULT OR PUP?

Whether to buy a grown dog or a small puppy is another question. It is undeniably fun to watch your dog grow all the way from a baby, sprawling and playful, to a mature, dignified dog. If you don't have the time to spend on the more frequent meals, housebreaking, and other training a puppy needs in order to become a dog you can be proud of, then choose an older, partly trained pup or a grown dog. If you want a show dog, remember that no one, not even an expert, can predict with 100 per cent accuracy what a small puppy will be when he grows up.

WORMING AND INOCULATION

Before you take your puppy home, find out from the breeder if he has already been wormed or inoculated for distemper and rabies. Practically all puppies will have worms which they acquire from eating worm eggs, from fleas, or from their mother. The breeder usually gives the puppies a worming before he sells them. If yours has already been wormed, find out when and what treatment was given. The breeder may be able to advise you on any further treatment that is necessary. While there are many commercial worming preparations on the market, it's generally safer to let the vet handle it. There will be more about worms in Chapter 3.

If your puppy has been inoculated against distemper, you will also have to know when this was done so you can give the information to your vet. He will complete the series of shots. If your puppy has not yet been given this protection, your vet should take care of it immediately. Distemper is highly prevalent and contagious. Don't let your puppy out of doors until he has had his distemper shots and they have had time to take effect.

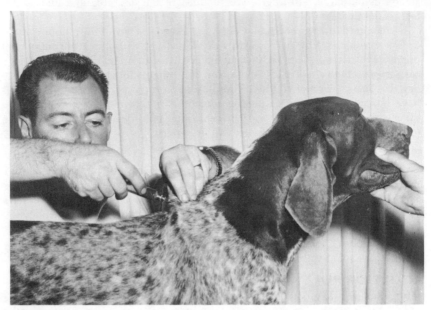

Check to see whether your town requires inoculation against rabies. If not, you may decide to dispense with it, as the chance that your Shorthair will become infected is very slight. However, be sure your dog is well protected against distemper.

As a rule, kennels and breeders do not inoculate puppies against rabies. In some areas, rabies inoculation is required by law. However, the possibility of your dog becoming affected with rabies, a contact disease, is very slight in most parts of the country. To be perfectly safe, check with your vet who will be familiar with the local ordinances and will advise you.

While the distemper inoculation is permanent and can be supplemented by "booster" shots, rabies inoculation must be repeated yearly. When your puppy receives it, the vet will give you a tag for the dog's collar certifying that he has received the protection. He will also give you a certificate for your own records. For foreign travel and some interstate travel, rabies inoculation is required.

3. Caring for Your German Shorthaired Pointer

BRINGING YOUR PUPPY HOME

When you bring your puppy home, remember that he is used to the peace and relative calm of a life of sleeping, eating and playing with his brothers and sisters. The trip away from all this is an adventure in itself, and so is adapting to a new home. So let him take it easy for a while. Don't let the whole neighborhood pat and poke him at one time. Be particularly careful when children want to handle him, for they cannot understand the difference between the delicate living puppy and the toy dog they play with and maul. Show them the correct way to hold the puppy, supporting his belly with one hand while holding him securely with the other.

THE PUPPY'S BED

It is up to you to decide where the puppy will sleep. He should have his own place, and not be allowed to climb all over the furniture. He should sleep out of drafts, but not right next to the heat, which would make him too sensitive to the cold when he goes outside.

You might partition off a section of a room—the kitchen is good because it's usually warm and he'll have some companionship there. Set up some sort of low partition that he can't climb, give him a pillow or old blanket for his bed and cover the floor with a thick layer of newspapers. If he seems a bit timid or retiring, get a sturdy cardboard box, cut a large door in one side and put his bed in there.

You have already decided where the puppy will sleep before you bring him home. Let him stay there, or in the corner he will soon learn is "his," most of the time, so that he will gain a sense of security from the familiar. Give the puppy a little food when he arrives, but don't worry if he isn't hungry at first. He will soon develop an appetite when he grows accustomed to his surroundings. The first night the puppy may cry a bit from lonesomeness, but if he has an old blanket or rug to curl up in he will be cozy. In winter a hot water bottle will help replace the warmth of his littermates, or the ticking of a clock may provide company.

FEEDING THE PUPPY

By the time a puppy is 8 weeks old, he should be fully weaned and eating from a dish. Always find out what the seller has been feeding the puppy as it is well to keep him on the same diet for a while. Any sudden change in a puppy's feeding habits may cause loose bowels or constipation.

The following feeding schedule has been used on many Shorthairs with good results.

WEANING TO 3 MONTHS: *A.M.*—$\frac{1}{2}$ cup of baby cereal and dog meal, mixed with warm water or milk. *Noon*—$\frac{1}{2}$ cup of warm milk, with cereal or biscuits. *P.M.*—2 tbs. chopped beef, 2 tbs. cereal or dog meal, vitamin and mineral supplements. *Bedtime*—$\frac{1}{2}$ cup warm milk, mixed with $\frac{1}{4}$ cup baby cereal. Change gradually from baby cereal to dog meal.

3-6 MONTHS: *A.M.*—$\frac{1}{2}$ cup meat, with shredded wheat or cereal. *Noon*—1 cup milk, soft-boiled egg twice a week, or 1 cup cottage cheese. *P.M.*—$\frac{1}{2}$ cup meat with $\frac{1}{2}$ cup dog meal; or kibble and water.

6 MONTHS-1 YEAR: *A.M.*—$\frac{1}{2}$ cup dog meal or cereal with cottage cheese or egg, and milk. Add vitamin and mineral supplements. *P.M.*—$\frac{1}{2}$ cup meat with $\frac{3}{4}$ cup kibble or meal, fat, table scraps.

The puppy's eating behavior is your best cue as to whether he needs more or less at each meal. Allow him a reasonable time—about ten minutes—to clean up his food. If he leaves food, give him a slightly smaller portion next time; if he finishes all you put out and keeps licking his dish, increase the portion. Use your own good judgment.

A dog that is over one year old should be given one substantial meal daily. It does not matter whether it is in the morning, during the day, or in the evening, but try always to feed him at about the same time. Remember that a dog who sits around the house requires less food than one that works hard in the field.

Like other members of the family, your German Shorthair should have his own "dining area." Feed him at the same time each day and, if you have a new pup, it's a good idea to keep him on whatever diet he's used to, at least for a while.

ADDITIONAL FEEDING TIPS

Occasional diarrhea in puppies may come from a change in food; if it persists, see your veterinarian.

Raw meat is considered better than cooked, but if your dog is ill, you should cook his meat. In any case, the food should be served at room temperature, never hot or cold.

As to the kind of meat, the lower-priced ground beef is preferable to the more expensive leaner cuts, since it contains a lot of fat that your dog needs in his diet. All kinds of liver, kidney, brains, and so forth are good. Of course you won't let your dog near chicken bones or fish with bones that can catch in his throat or tear his intestines. It is usually best not to feed him pork, fried meats or over-spiced foods.

Cream and cottage cheese are relished by most dogs and are nutritious. In addition, cottage cheese may stop mild diarrhea.

Green and yellow vegetables, cooked, are desirable dog foods, but some dogs react unfavorably to peas, onions and garlic. Cooked or raw fruit may be given, and while authorities agree that dogs do not need the Vitamin C in citrus foods, an occasional piece of orange or grapefruit may please your dog.

If you buy canned dog food, study the label carefully and make certain that it contains a large proportion of meat. The lower-priced foods are frequently overloaded with cereal and are low in protein content. If you feed dried food, add beef fat or bacon drippings.

A day or two without food won't harm a healthy dog. Many kennels "starve" their dogs one day a week, claiming that this keeps them more active and alert.

WATCHING THE PUPPY'S HEALTH

The first step in protecting the health of your puppy is a visit to the veterinarian. If the breeder has not given your puppy his first distemper shots, have your vet do it. You should also have your dog protected against hepatitis, and, if required by local law or if your vet suggests it, against rabies. Your puppy should receive his full quota of protective inoculations, especially if you plan to show him later. Select a veterinarian you feel you can trust and keep his phone number handy. Any vet will be glad to give a regular "patient" advice over the phone—often without charge.

Occasional loose bowels in a puppy generally isn't anything too serious. It can be the result of an upset stomach or a slight cold. Sometimes it will clear up in a day or so without any treatment. If you want to help the puppy's digestion, add some cottage cheese to his diet, or give him a few drops of kaopectate. Instead of tap water, give him barley or oatmeal water (just as you would a human baby). However, if the looseness persists for more than a day or two, a visit to the vet may be required. If the puppy has normal bowel movements alternating with loose bowel movements, it may be a symptom of worms.

If the puppy upchucks a meal or vomits up slime or white froth, it may indicate that his stomach is upset. One good stomach-settler is a pinch of baking soda, or about 4 or 5 drops of pure witch hazel in a teaspoon of cold water two or three times a day. In case of vomiting you should skip a few meals to give the stomach a chance to clear itself out. When you start to feed him again, give him cooked scraped beef for his first meals and then return to his normal diet. Persistent vomiting may indicate a serious stomach upset or even poisoning and calls for professional help.

WORMING

Practically all puppies start out life with worms in their insides, either acquired from the mother or picked up in their sleeping quarters. However, there are six different types of worms. Some will be visible in the stool as small white objects; others require microscopic examination of the stool for identification. While there are many commercial worm remedies on the market, it is safest to leave that to your veterinarian, and to follow his instructions on feeding the puppy before and after the worming. If you find that you must administer a worm remedy yourself, read the directions carefully and administer the smallest possible dose. Keep the puppy confined after treatment for worms, since many of the remedies have a strong laxative action and the puppy will soil the house if allowed to roam freely.

THE USEFUL THERMOMETER

Almost every serious puppy ailment shows itself by an increase in the puppy's body temperature. If your young dog acts lifeless, looks dull-eyed and gives an impression of illness, check by using a rectal thermometer. Hold the dog, insert the thermometer which has been lubricated with vaseline and take a reading. The normal temperature is 100.6 to 101.5 (higher than the normal human temperature). Excitement may send it up slightly, but any rise of more than a few points is cause for alarm.

SOME CANINE DISEASES

Amateur diagnosis is dangerous because the symptoms of so many dog diseases are alike, but you should be familiar with some of the more prevalent ones which can strike your dog.

COUGHS, COLDS, BRONCHITIS, PNEUMONIA

Respiratory diseases may affect the dog because he is forced to live in a human rather than a natural doggy environment. Being subjected to a draft or cold after a bath, sleeping near an air conditioner or in the path of air from a fan or near a hot air register or radiator can cause one of these respiratory ailments. The symptoms are similar to those in humans. However, the germs of these diseases are different and do not affect both dogs and humans so that they cannot catch them from each other. Treatment is pretty much the same as for a child with the same illness. Keep the puppy warm, quiet, well fed. Your veterinarian has antibiotics and other remedies to help the pup fight back.

If your puppy gets wet, dry him immediately to guard against chilling. Wipe his stomach after he has walked through damp grass. Don't make the common mistake of running your dog to the vet every time he sneezes. If he seems to have a light cold, give him an aspirin tablet and see that he doesn't overexercise.

If you treat him well and keep him in good health, your Shorthaired Pointer will be appreciative and affectionate. His sturdy, well-balanced body and animated manner will reflect his excellent physical condition.

MAJOR DISEASES OF THE DOG

With the proper series of inoculations, your Shorthair will be almost completely protected against the following canine diseases. However, it occasionally happens that the shot doesn't take and sometimes a different form of the virus appears against which your dog may not be protected.

Rabies. This is an acute disease of the dog's central nervous system and is spread by the bite of an infected animal, the saliva carrying the infection. Rabies occurs in two forms. The first is "Furious Rabies" in which the dog shows a period of melancholy or depression, then irritation, and finally paralysis. The first period lasts from a few hours to several days. During this time the dog is cross and will try to hide from members of the family. He appears restless and will change his position often. He loses his appetite for food and begins to lick, bite and swallow foreign objects. During the "irritation" phase the dog is spasmodically wild and has impulses to run away. He acts in a fearless manner and runs and bites at everything in sight. If he is caged or confined he will fight at the bars, often breaking teeth or fracturing his jaw. His bark becomes a peculiar howl. In the final or paralysis stage, the animal's lower jaw becomes paralyzed and hangs down; he walks with a stagger and saliva drips from his mouth. Within four to eight days after the onset of paralysis, the dog dies.

The second form of rabies, "Dumb Rabies," is characterized by the dog's walking in a bear-like manner with his head down. The lower jaw is paralyzed and the dog is unable to bite. Outwardly it may seem as though he has a bone caught in his throat.

Even if your pet should be bitten by a rabid dog or other animal, he can probably be saved if you get him to the vet in time for a series of injections. However, by the time the symptoms appear the disease is so far advanced that no cure is possible. But remember that an annual rabies inoculation is almost certain protection against rabies.

Distemper: Young dogs are most susceptible to distemper, although it may affect dogs of all ages. The dog will lose his appetite, seem depressed, chilled, and run a fever. Often he will have a watery discharge from his eyes and nose. Unless treated promptly, the disease goes into advanced stages with infections of the lungs, intestines and nervous system, and dogs that recover may be left with some impairment such as a twitch or other nervous mannerism. The best protection against this is very early inoculation—preferably even before the puppy is old enough to go out into the street and meet other dogs.

Hepatitis: Veterinarians report an increase in the spread of this virus disease in recent years, usually with younger dogs as the victims. The initial symptoms— drowsiness, vomiting, great thirst, loss of appetite and a high temperature— closely resemble distemper. These symptoms are often accompanied by swellings on the head, neck and lower parts of the belly. The disease strikes quickly and death may occur in a few hours. Protection is afforded by injection with a new vaccine.

Leptospirosis: This disease is caused by bacteria which live in stagnant or slow-moving water. It is carried by rats and dogs, and many dogs are believed to get it from licking the urine or feces of infected rats. The symptoms are increased thirst, depression and weakness. In the acute stage, there is vomiting, diarrhea and a brown discoloration of the jaws, tongue and teeth, caused by an inflammation of the kidneys. This disease can be cured if caught in time, but it is best to ward it off with a vaccine which your vet can administer along with the distemper shots.

External Parasites: The dog that is groomed regularly and provided with clean sleeping quarters should not be troubled with fleas, ticks or lice. However, it would be a wise precaution to spray his sleeping quarters occasionally with an anti-parasite powder that you can get at your pet shop or from your vet. If the dog is out of doors during the tick season he should be treated with a dip-bath.

Skin Ailments: Any persistent scratching may indicate an irritation, and whenever you groom your dog, look for the reddish spots that may indicate eczema or some rash or.fungus infection. Rather than treating him yourself, take him to the veterinarian as some of the conditions may be difficult to eradicate and can cause permanent harm to his coat.

FIRST AID FOR YOUR DOG

In general, a dog will lick his cuts and wounds and they'll heal. If he swallows anything harmful, chances are he'll throw it up. But it will probably make you feel better to help him if he's hurt, so treat his wounds as you would your own. Wash out the dirt and apply an antiseptic or ointment. If you put on a bandage, you'll have to do something to keep the dog from trying to remove it. A large cardboard ruff around his neck will prevent him from licking his chest or body. You can tape up his nails to keep him from scratching, or make "booties" for his paws.

If you think your dog has a broken bone, before moving him apply a splint just as you would to a person's limb. If there is bleeding that won't stop, apply a tourniquet between the wound and heart, but loosen it every few minutes to prevent damage to the circulatory system.

If you are afraid that your dog has swallowed poison and you can't get the vet fast enough, try to induce vomiting by giving him a strong solution of salt water or mustard in water.

SOME "BUTS"

First, don't be frightened by the number of diseases a dog can get. The majority of dogs never get any of them. If you need assurance, look at any book on human diseases. How many have you had?

Don't become a dog-hypochondriac. Veterinarians have enough work taking care of sick dogs and doing preventive work with their patients. Don't rush your pet to the vet every time he sneezes or seems tired. All dogs have days on which they feel lazy and want to lie around doing nothing.

THE FEMALE PUPPY

If you want to spay your female you can have it done while she is still a puppy. Her first seasonal period will probably occur between eight and ten months, although it may be as early as six or delayed until she is a year old. She may be spayed before or after this, or you may breed her (at a later season) and still spay her afterward.

The first sign of the female's being in season is a thin red discharge, which will increase for about a week, when it changes color to a thin yellowish stain, lasting about another week. Simultaneously there is a swelling of the vulva, the dog's external sexual organ. The second week is the crucial period, when she could be bred if you wanted her to have puppies, but it is possible for the period to be shorter or longer, so it is best not to take unnecessary risks at any time. After a third week the swelling decreases and the period is over for about six months.

If you have an absolutely climb-proof and dig-proof run within your yard, it will be safe to leave her there, but otherwise the female in season should be shut indoors. Don't leave her out alone for even a minute; she should be exercised only on leash. If you want to prevent the neighborhood dogs from hanging around your doorstep, as they inevitably will as soon as they discover that your female is in season, take her some distance away from the house before you let her relieve herself. Take her in the car to a nearby park or field for a chance to stretch her legs. After the three weeks are up you can let her out as before, with no worry that she can have puppies until the next season. But if you want to have her spayed, consult your veterinarian about the time and age at which he prefers to do it. With a young dog the operation is simple and after a night or two at the animal hospital she can be at home, wearing only a small bandage as a souvenir.

GROOMING YOUR GERMAN SHORTHAIRED POINTER

The ease of grooming the Shorthair is another point in his favor. He has a tight, short coat which does not hold burrs and does not tangle or form hair knots. With proper food—including an adequate amount of fats (about 8 per cent)—exercise and a brushing once in a while to get rid of dead hairs, your dog should have a good coat and there should be practically no shedding around the house. Many handlers use a "hound" glove to work on the short coat. This is a sort of combination of glove and mitten, and is available in most pet shops.

CARING FOR THE COAT

Start each grooming session with a brisk rubdown with your finger tips over the dog's whole body. This will loosen any dead skin. Then give him a thorough but gentle brushing. (A natural bristle brush is preferable to the nylon type.) First brush his coat against the grain, then with the grain. When you brush him, especially during the summer and fall months, check his coat for any signs of fleas, lice or ticks. If you do find parasites, use a spray or dip to get rid of them. When there are fleas, you will also have to change the dog's bedding and spray the areas of the house where he stays, paying special attention to cracks in the floor and along the baseboards. Repeat the de-fleaing treatment in about a week. Make sure the dog doesn't lick too much insecticide off his coat; if necessary, you can put a clown collar around his neck so he won't be able to reach his body with his tongue. Don't leave flea powder on too long, as it may be strong enough to burn his skin or coat.

If you find ticks, be sure to remove the entire insects. You can touch them with a drop of iodine to break their grip. Then lift them off, one at a time, with a pair of tweezers or a tissue and burn them or drop them into kerosene or gasoline to kill them.

If you find lice, small sucking and biting insects which attach themselves to the dog's body, you must apply a good pesticide regularly, burn all the dog's bedding and thoroughly disinfect his living quarters.

BATHING YOUR SHORTHAIR

A normal, healthy dog should be bathed as *infrequently* as possible because the dog's skin is different from that of humans. It is very rich in oil glands and deficient in sweat glands. The oil keeps his skin soft and prevents it from drying and cracking. It also protects the coat and keeps it water-resistant.

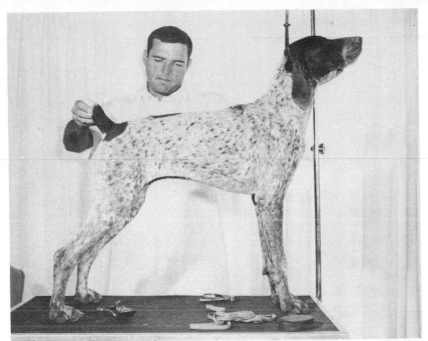

Grooming your Shorthair is relatively easy, because his close-growing, straight coat will not tangle, nor will the dog shed on good furniture and clothing. For brushing sessions, you can keep him standing still by attaching his leash to a point above his head.

When a dog is bathed too often, the natural oil is removed from his skin and the skin and coat become dry. Minute cracks in the skin cause irritation, the dog scratches and bites himself and eczema or other infectious skin ailments may result.

So bathe your dog only when he gets so dirty that it is impossible to clean him any other way. When a bath is necessary, protect the dog's eyes and ears from water before putting him into the tub. Put a drop of castor oil into each eye and plug his ears with cotton. The water should be lukewarm, never hot or cold. Use a special dog soap which does not contain much alkali and rinse all traces of soap from his coat. Then dry him with a thick towel, massage his coat with your hand and brush him. If the day is warm and sunny, let him run outdoors to complete the drying, but if it is cold keep him indoors.

WATCH THE TOENAILS

Many dogs that run on gravel or pavements keep their toenails down, so they seldom need clipping. But a dog that doesn't do much running, or runs on grass, will grow long toenails that can be harmful. The long nails will force the dog's toes into the air and spread his feet wide. In addition, the nails may force the dog into an unnatural stance that may produce lameness.

You can control your dog's toenails by cutting them with a special dog

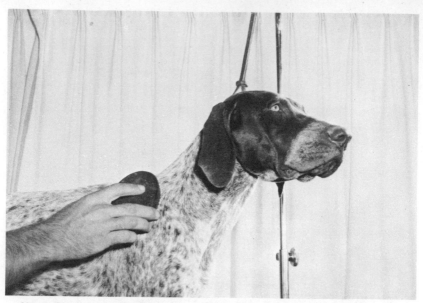

Above: After rubbing him down with your finger tips to loosen dead skin, brush your Shorthair, first against the grain, then with it. A natural bristle brush is better for this purpose than one with nylon bristles.

Below: If your German Shorthair is not a professional in the ring, grooming will be simple. But if your dog is a champion you will want to add special grooming touches, for example, a careful trimming job on the legs.

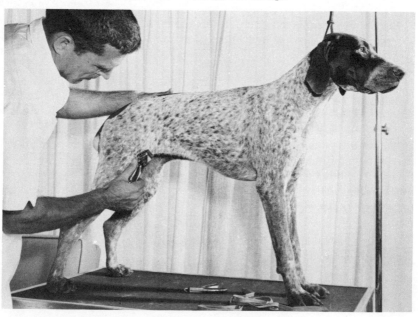

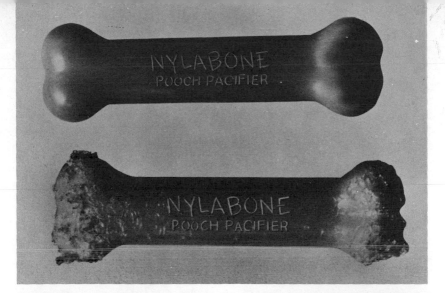

NYLABONE® is a necessity that is available at your local petshop (not in supermarkets). The puppy or grown dog chews the hambone flavored nylon into a frilly dog toothbrush, massaging his gums and cleaning his teeth as he plays. Veterinarians highly recommend this product . . . but beware of cheap imitations which might splinter or break.

clipper or by filing them. Many dogs object to the clipping and it takes some experience to learn just how to do it without cutting into the blood vessels. Your vet will probably examine your dog's nails whenever you bring him in and will trim them at no extra charge. He can show you how to do it yourself in the future. If you prefer, you can file the points off your dog's nails every few weeks with a flat wooden file. Draw the file in only one direction—from the top of the nail downward in a round stroke to the end of the nail or underneath. You'll need considerable pressure for the first few strokes to break through the hard, polished surface, but then it gets easier.

Incidentally, it's a good idea to keep your young puppy from walking on waxed or slippery floors, as this tends to break down the pasterns.

EYES, EARS AND TEETH

If you notice matter collecting in the corners of the dog's eyes, wipe it out with a piece of cotton or tissue. If there is a discharge, check with your vet.

If your Shorthair has been working in the field, you should watch his eyes carefully. Sometimes weeds or other foreign materials get caught under the eyelids and must be removed. Some owners make it a habit to wash out the dog's eyes with a mild boric acid solution on returning from a hunt or field trip.

During every grooming session, brush your Shorthair's ear flaps to remove any matted dirt or food. Examine the ears and remove all visible wax, using a piece of cotton dipped in a boric acid solution or a solution of equal parts of water and hydrogen peroxide. Be gentle and don't probe into the ear, but just clean the parts you can see. If your dog constantly shakes his head, twitches his ears or scratches them, it is best to have the vet take a look.

Shorthaired Pointers are sporting dogs. They need a great deal of exercise and activity. If possible, let your dog run and play much of the day with other dogs or with the neighborhood children.

If you give your dog a hard chewing bone—the kind you can buy at a pet store—it will serve him as your toothbrush serves you and will prevent the accumulation of tartar on his teeth. However, check his mouth occasionally and take him to the vet if you find collected tartar or bloody spots on his gums.

EXERCISE

Remember always that the German Shorthaired Pointer is a sporting dog of the outdoor type rather than strictly a house dog. Unless you give him the exercise he needs you are shortening his life. A dog will "soften up" and acquire unhealthy internal fat much faster than a human under the same circumstances. A walk a few times a day on a leash is *not* sufficient for the Shorthair. He should be free to run about at will for a good portion of the day. He will get enough exercise in a rural or suburban area, especially if he has the company of children or other dogs. If you must keep him in a kennel, or fenced-in area, let him out for at least an hour daily to give him a chance to stretch his muscles. It is suggested that he wait at least two hours after his big meal of the day for his "run" and that in hot weather he be given a chance to run about either in the cooler morning or evening hours.

If you are planning to work your Shorthair in the field, you should start at least a month before the hunting season to get him in shape with progressively longer runs, and it may do you good to get in shape along with him.

4. Housebreaking and Training Your German Shorthaired Pointer

The first months of your puppy's life will be a busy time. While he's getting his preventive shots and becoming acquainted with his new family, he should learn the elements of housebreaking that will make him a welcome addition to your home and community.

HOUSEBREAKING THE PUPPY

Housebreaking the puppy isn't difficult because his natural instinct is to keep the place where he sleeps and plays clean. The most important factor is to keep him confined to a fairly small area during the training period. You will find it almost impossible to housebreak a puppy who is given free run of the house. After months of yelling and screaming, you may finally get it through his head that the parlor rug is "verboten," but it will be a long, arduous process.

FIRST, PAPER TRAINING

Spread papers over the puppy's living area. Then watch him carefully. When you notice him starting to whimper, sniff the ground or run around in agitated little circles, rush him to the place that you want to serve as his "toilet" and hold him there till he does his business. Then praise him lavishly. When you remove the soiled papers, leave a small damp piece so that the puppy's sense of smell will lead him back there next time. If he makes a mistake, wash it immediately with warm water, followed by a rinse with water and vinegar. That will kill the odor and prevent discoloration.

It shouldn't take more than a few days for the puppy to get the idea of using newspaper. When he becomes fairly consistent, reduce the area of paper to a few sheets in a corner. As soon as you think he has the idea fixed in his mind, you can let him roam around the house a bit, but keep an eye on him. It might be best to keep him on leash the first few days so you can rush him back to his paper at any signs of an approaching accident.

The normally healthy puppy will want to relieve himself when he wakes up in the morning, after each feeding and after strenuous exercise. During early puppyhood any excitement, such as the return home of a member of the family or the approach of a visitor, may result in floor-wetting, but that phase should pass in a few weeks.

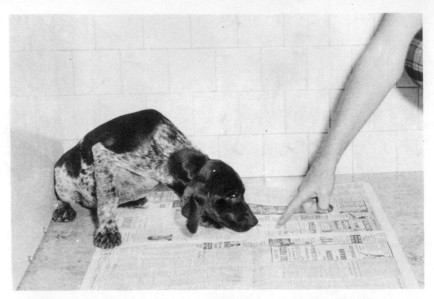

Paper training is quickly grasped by the intelligent Shorthair. Always keep newspapers on the floor of his living area. Praise him when he performs in the right spot. In the beginning it helps to leave a scrap of soiled newspaper for scent after you have removed most of the used ones.

OUTDOOR HOUSEBREAKING

Keep in mind during the housebreaking process that you can't expect too much from your puppy until he is about 5 months old. Before that, his muscles and digestive system just aren't under his control. However, you can begin outdoor training even while you are paper training the puppy. (He should have learned to walk on lead at this point. See page 34.) First thing in the morning, take him outdoors (to the curb if you are in a city) and walk him back and forth in a small area until he relieves himself. He will probably make a puddle and then just walk around uncertain of what is expected of him. You can try standing him over a piece of newspaper which may give him the idea. Some dog trainers use glycerine suppositories at this point for fast action. Praise the dog every time taking him outside brings results and he'll get the idea. After each meal take him to the same spot.

Use some training word to help your puppy learn. Pick a word that you won't use for any other command and repeat it while you are walking your dog in his outdoor "business" area. It will be a big help when the dog is older if you have some word of command that he can connect with approval to relieve himself in a strange place. You'll find, when you begin the outdoor training, that the male puppy usually requires a longer walk than the female. Both male and female puppies will squat. It isn't until he's quite a bit older that the male dog will begin to lift his leg.

NIGHTTIME TRAINING

If you hate to give up any sleep, you can train your new Shorthair puppy to go outdoors during the day and use the paper at night for the first few months. After he's older, he'll be able to contain himself all night and wait for his first morning walk. However, if you want to speed up the outdoor training so that you can leave the dog alone in the house with less fear of an accident, keep him confined at night so that he has enough room to move around in his bed but not enough to get any distance away from it. When he has to go, he'll whine loudly enough to attract your attention. Then take him or let him out. You may have to get up once or twice a night for a few weeks but then you can be fairly sure that your puppy will behave indoors—although accidents will happen. Sometimes even a grown dog will suddenly—and for no apparent reason—soil the house, usually the most expensive carpet in it.

Occasionally a puppy that seems to have been housebroken will revert to indiscriminate acts all over the place. If that happens it may be necessary to go back to the beginning and repeat the paper training.

WHEN HE MISBEHAVES

Rubbing a puppy's nose in his dirt or whacking him with a newspaper may make you feel better, but it won't help train the puppy. A dog naturally *wants* to do the right thing for his master. Your job is to show him what you want. If an accident happens, ignore it unless you can catch him immediately and then in a firm tone express your displeasure and take him to the spot he should have used. A puppy has a short memory span, and bawling him out for something that happened a half-hour before will have no meaning to him. When he does use the right place, be lavish with praise and petting, but first be sure he has finished. Many a puppy has left a trail of water across a floor because someone interrupted him to tell him how well he was doing.

PUPPY DISCIPLINE

A 6- or 8-week-old puppy is old enough to understand what is probably the most important word in his vocabulary—"NO!" The first time you see the puppy doing something he shouldn't do, chewing something he shouldn't chew or wandering in a forbidden area, it's time to teach him. Shout "No" and stamp your foot, hit the table with a piece of newspaper or make some other loud noise. Dogs, especially very young ones, don't like loud noises and your misbehaving pet will readily connect the word with something unpleasant. If he persists, repeat the "No," hold him firmly and slap him sharply across the nose. Before you protest to the A.S.P.C.A. you should realize that a dog does not resent being disciplined if he is doing something wrong and is caught in the act. However, do not chase a puppy around while waving a rolled-up newspaper at him or trying to swat him. Punish him only when you have a firm hold on him. Above all, never call him to you and then punish him. He must learn to associate coming to you with something pleasant.

Every puppy will pick things up. So the second command should be "Drop it!" or "Let go!" Don't engage in a tug-of-war with the puppy, but take the forbidden object from him even if you have to pry his jaws open with your fingers. Many dogs will release what they are holding if you just blow sharply into their faces. Let your dog know that you are displeased when he picks up something he shouldn't.

If you give him toys of his own, he will be less liable to chew your possessions. Avoid soft rubber toys that he can chew to pieces. Don't give him cloth toys, either, as he'll probably swallow pieces and have trouble getting them out of his system. Skip the temptation to give him an old slipper, because it will be hard for him to distinguish between that and a brand-new pair you certainly won't want him to chew. Your pet shop will have some indestructible toys that will be fine for your German Shorthaired Pointer.

However, even with training, reconcile yourself to the fact that during puppyhood things will be chewed and damaged, but that's a passing phase in the growth of a dog.

CLIMBING ON FURNITURE

If your puppy shows a fondness for climbing on furniture, this is another habit you'll have to break early. The upholstery holds the scent of the people he likes, and besides, it's more comfortable than the hard floor or even the carpet. Sometimes verbal corrections will be enough to establish the fact that the furniture is taboo. If not, try putting crinkly cellophane on the furniture to keep him off. If that doesn't work, you can get liquids at your pet store that you can't smell, but whose odor keeps the dog off.

A firm "No" will make your dog understand that he's out of line. Appealing as table begging may seem at first, eventually this habit will turn your dog into a nuisance. Don't let him become a glutton or a moocher.

5. Obedience Training for Your German Shorthaired Pointer

The purpose of obedience training is not to turn your dog into a puppet but to make him a civilized member of the community in which he will live, and to keep him safe. This training is most important as it makes the difference between having an undisciplined animal in the house or having an enjoyable companion. Both you and your dog will learn a lot from training.

HOW A DOG LEARNS

The dog is the one domestic animal that seems to want to do what his master asks. Unlike other animals that learn by fear or rewards, the dog will work willingly if he is given a kind word or a show of affection. The Shorthair is particularly receptive to training.

The hardest part of dog training is communication. If you can get across to the dog what you want him to do, he'll do it. Always remember that your dog does not understand the English language. He can, however, interpret your tone of voice and your gestures. By associating certain words with the act that accompanies them, the dog can acquire a fairly large working vocabulary. Keep in mind that it is the sound rather than the meaning of the words that the dog understands. When he doesn't respond properly, let him know by the tone of your voice that you are disappointed, but follow each correction with a show of affection.

YOUR PART IN TRAINING

You must patiently demonstrate to your dog what each simple word of command means. Guide him with your hands and the training leash through whatever routine you are teaching him. Repeat the word associated with the act. Demonstrate again and again to give the dog the chance to make the connection in his mind. (In psychological language, you are conditioning him to give a specific response to a specific stimulus.)

Once he begins to get the idea, use the word of command without any physical guidance. Drill him. When he makes mistakes, correct him, kindly at first, more severely as his training progresses. Try not to lose your patience or become irritated, and never slap him with your hand or the leash during a training session. Withholding praise or rebuking him will make him feel badly enough.

When he does what you want, praise him lavishly with words and with pats. Don't rely on dog candy or treats in training. The dog that gets into the habit of performing for treats will seldom be fully dependable when he can't smell or see one in the offing. When he carries out a command, even though his performance is slow or sloppy, praise him and he will perform more readily the next time.

THE TRAINING VOICE

When you start training your dog student, use your training voice, giving commands in a firm, clear tone. Once you give the command, persist until it is obeyed even if you have to pull the dog protestingly to obey you. He must learn that training is different from playing, that a command once given must be obeyed no matter what distractions are present. Remember that the tone and sound of your voice, not loudness, are the qualities that will influence your dog.

Be consistent in the use of words during training. Confine your commands to as few words as possible and never change them. It is best for only one person to carry on the dog's training because different people will use different words and tactics that will confuse the animal. The dog who hears "come," "get over here," "hurry up," "here, Rover," and other commands when he is wanted will become totally confused.

TAKE IT EASY

Training is hard on the dog—and on the trainer. A young dog just cannot take more than 10 minutes of training at a stretch, so limit the length of your first lessons. You'll find that you, too, will tend to become impatient when you stretch out a training session, and losing your temper won't help either of you. Before and after each lesson have a play period, but don't play during a training session. Even the youngest dog soon learns that schooling is a serious matter; fun comes afterward.

Never rely on edible rewards during obedience training. The elements of training are simple—a leash, a firm, clear voice for giving commands, lavish praise for the dog when he responds correctly and a great deal of patience on your part. Always let your pup tear around and play between training sessions.

"Sorry, Boss"—that's what this Shorthair's "hangdog" look seems to say. It's easy to understand why your dog longs for a soft seat in a chair. No doubt about it, chairs are more comfortable than the floor. But, as you will have to point out, the floor is the place for dogs.

Don't spend too much time on one phase of training or the dog will become bored. And always try to end a training session on a pleasant note. If the dog doesn't seem to be getting what you are trying to show him, go back to something simpler that he can do. This way you will end every lesson with a pleasant feeling of accomplishment. Actually, in nine cases out of ten, if your dog isn't doing what you want, it's because you're not getting the idea over to him properly.

WALKING ON LEAD

"Doggy" people call the leash a "lead," so we'll use that term here. With your Shorthair, don't go in for any kind of fancy lead or collar. The best lead for training purposes is the 6-foot webbed-cloth lead, usually olive-drab in color.

As for the collar, you'll need a metal-link collar called a "choke" collar. Even though the name may sound frightening, it won't hurt your dog and it's an absolute *must* in training. It tightens when you snap the lead, eases when you relax your grip. It's important to put the collar on properly. Slide the chain around your dog's neck so that you can attach the lead to the ring at the end of the chain which passes *over*, not under, his neck.

Put the collar and lead on the puppy and let him walk around the house first with the lead dragging on the floor. This is just to let him get the feel of the strange object around his neck. But a word of caution for afterward: don't let the dog wander around with the choke collar on. If it's loose he'll lose it, and it's possible for it to catch on any projection and choke him. For his license tag and rabies tag you can get a light leather collar that fits more snugly.

A lead is indispensable in training. Hold it as shown here, in your right hand, letting it pass through the left so that you can jerk it when you want to give the dog a correction or bring him closer to your left side.

When teaching your Shorthaired Pointer to sit, keep the lead rather short. As you give the command, pull the lead up slightly. At first, you may have to push down on the dog's hindquarters.

Now, here's a lesson for you. From the start, hold the lead firmly in your right hand. Keep the dog at your left side. You can use your left hand to jerk the lead when necessary to give corrections or to bring the dog closer to you. Do not *pull* on the lead. Give it a sharp snap when you want to correct the dog, and then release it. The dog cannot learn from being pulled around. He will learn when he finds that doing certain things results in a sharp jerk; doing other things allows him to walk comfortably on lead.

At first, the puppy will fight the lead. He'll probably plant all four feet or his rear end on the ground and wait for your next move. Be patient. Short tugs on the lead will help him learn his part in walking with you. If he gets overexcited, calm him before taking off the lead and collar and picking him up. He must learn there's nothing to fear. (Incidentally, if the lesson is being given on a city street, it might be a good idea to carry some paper to clean up the mess he may leave in his excitement.)

TRAINING TO SIT

Training your dog to sit should be fairly easy. Stand him on your left side, holding the lead fairly short, and command him to "Sit." As you give the verbal command, pull up slightly with the lead and push his hindquarters down (you may have to kneel to do this). Do not let him lie down or stand up. Keep him in a sitting position for a moment, then release the pressure on the lead and praise him. Constantly repeat the command word as you hold him in a sitting position, thus fitting the word to the action in his mind. After a while,

You will be proud of your German Shorthair's aristocratic appearance once he has mastered the "stand." He should remain in one place without moving until given a command, and should not become nervous or resentful if strangers touch him. The only difficulty in teaching your Shorthair to stand is that at first he may confuse this command with the one which means "sit." You can prevent him from sitting by wrapping the lead around his hindquarters.

A special winning trait of this combined hunter and housedog is his gentleness and loyalty toward children. You will find your German Shorthair non-aggressive. His patience is almost unlimited. This means that he can take a lot of abuse from loving but rough youngsters. In every way, this dog will be a treasured addition to your family.

he will begin to get the idea and will sit without your having to push his back down. When he reaches that stage, insist that he sit on command. If he is slow to obey, slap his hindquarters with the end of the lead to get him down fast. Teach him to sit on command facing you as well as when he is at your side. When he begins sitting on command with the lead on, try it with the lead off.

THE "LIE DOWN"

The object of this is to get the dog to lie down either on the verbal command "Down!" or when you give him a hand signal, your hand raised, palm toward the dog—a sort of threatening gesture. This is one of the most important parts of training. A well-trained dog will drop on command and stay down whatever the temptation—car-chasing, cat-chasing, or another dog across the street.

Don't start this until the dog is almost letter-perfect in sitting on command. Then, place the dog in a sit. Force him down by pulling his front feet out forward while pressing on his shoulders and repeating "Down!" Hold the dog down and stroke him gently to let him know that staying down is what you expect of him.

After he begins to get the idea, slide the lead under your left foot and give the command "Down!" At the same time, pull on the lead. This will help get the dog down. Meanwhile, raise your hand in the down signal. Don't expect to accomplish all this in one session. Be patient and work with the dog. He'll co-operate if you show him just what you expect him to do.

THE "STAY"

The next step is to train your dog to stay in either a "sit" or "down" position. Sit him at your side. Give him the command "Stay," but be careful not to use his name with that command as hearing his name may lead him to think that some action is expected of him. If he begins to move, repeat "Stay" firmly and hold him down in the sit. Constantly repeat the word "Stay" to fix the meaning of that command in his mind. When he stays for a short time, gradually increase the length of his stay. The hand signal for "Stay" is a downward sweep of your hand toward the dog's nose, with the palm toward him. While he is sitting, walk around him and stand in front of him. Hold the lead at first; later, drop the lead on the ground in front of him and keep him sitting. If he bolts, correct him severely and force him back to a sit in the same place.

Use some word such as "okay" or "up" to let him know when he can get up, and praise him well for a good performance. As this practice continues, walk farther and farther away from him. Later, try sitting him, giving him the command to stay, and then walk out of sight, first for a few seconds, then for longer periods. A well-trained dog should stay where you put him without moving for three minutes or more.

Similarly, practice having him stay in down position, first with you near him, later when you step out of sight.

THE "COME" ON COMMAND

A young puppy will come a-running to people, but an older puppy or dog will have other plans of his own when his master calls him. However, you can train your dog to come when you call him if you begin when he is young. At first, work with him on lead. Sit the dog, then back away the length of the lead and call him, putting as much coaxing affection in your voice as possible. Give an easy tug on the lead to get him started. When he does come, make a big fuss over him and it might help to hand him a piece of dog candy or food as a reward. He should get the idea soon. Then attach a long piece of cord to the lead—15 or 20 feet—and make him come to you from that distance. When he's coming pretty consistently, have him sit when he reaches you.

Don't be too eager to practice coming on command off lead. Wait till you are certain that you have the dog under perfect control before you try calling him when he's free. Once he gets the idea that he can disobey a command to come and get away with it, your training program will suffer a serious setback. Keep in mind that your dog's life may depend on his immediate response to a command to come when he is called. If he disobeys off lead, put the collar back on and correct him severely with jerks of the lead. He'll get the idea.

In training your dog to come, never use the command when you want to punish him. He should associate the "Come" with something pleasant. If he comes very slowly, you can speed his response by pulling on the lead, calling him and running backward with him at a brisk pace.

At first, practice the "sit," "down," "stay" and "come" indoors; then try it in an outdoor area where there are distractions to show the dog that he must obey under any conditions.

HEELING

"Heeling" in dog language means having your pet walk alongside you on your left side, close to your left leg, on lead or off. With patience and effort you can train your dog to walk with you even on a crowded street or in the presence of other dogs. However, don't begin this part of his training too early. Normally, a dog much under 6 months old is just too young to absorb the idea of heeling.

Put the dog at your left side, sitting. Then say "Heel" firmly and start walking at a brisk pace. Do not pull the dog with you, but guide him by tugs at the lead. Keep some slack on the lead and use your left hand to snap the lead for a correction. Always start off with your left foot and after a while the dog will learn to watch that foot and follow it. Keep repeating "Heel" as you walk, snapping the dog back into position if he lags behind or forges ahead. If he gets out of control, reverse your course sharply and snap him along after you. Keep up a running conversation with your dog, telling him what a good fellow he is when he is heeling, letting him know when he is not.

At first limit your heeling practice to about 5 minutes at a time; later extend it to 15 minutes or a half-hour. To keep your dog interested, vary the routine. Make right and left turns, change your pace from a normal walk to a fast trot to a very slow walk. Occasionally make a sharp about-face.

Remember to emphasize the word "Heel" throughout this practice and to use your voice to let him know that you are displeased when he goes ahead or drops behind or swings wide.

Unless it's impossible to get him clean otherwise, never bathe your German Shorthair. With regular, thorough grooming sessions, your dog will be clean, his coat in good condition, his general appearance handsome. However, if you live in an extremely warm climate and feel you MUST bathe your dog, it's safe to do it outdoors.

Follow your dog's bath with a brisk rubdown. Next, dry him thoroughly with heavy towels. Then give him a hand massage, followed by a good brushing. Make sure he stays in a warm place until he is thoroughly dry.

If you are handling him properly, the dog should begin to get the idea of heeling in about 15 minutes. If you get no response whatever, if the dog runs away from you, fights the lead, gets you and himself tangled in the lead, it may indicate that he is still young, or that you aren't showing him what you expect him to do.

Practicing 15 minutes a day, in 6 or 7 weeks your pet should have developed to the stage where you can remove the lead and he'll heel alongside you. First try throwing the lead over your shoulder or fastening it to your belt, or remove the lead and tie a piece of thin cord (fishing line will do nicely) to his collar. Then try him off lead. Keep his attention by constantly talking; slap your left leg to keep his attention on you. If he breaks away, return to the collar and lead treatment for a while.

"HEEL" MEANS SIT, TOO

To the dog, the command "Heel" will also mean that he has to sit in heel position at your left side when you stop walking—with no additional command from you. As you practice heeling, force him to sit whenever you stop, at first using the word "Sit," then switching over to the command "Heel." He'll soon get the idea and plop his rear end down when you stop and wait for you to give the command "Heel" and start walking again.

TEACHING TO COME TO HEEL

The object of this is for you to stand still, say "Heel!" and have your dog come right over to you and sit by your left knee in heel position. If your dog has been trained to sit without command every time you stop, he's ready for this step.

Sit him in front of and facing you and step back a few feet. Say "Heel" in your most commanding tone of voice and pull the dog into heel position, making him sit. There are several different ways to do this. You can swing the dog around behind you from your right side, behind your back and to heel position. Or you can pull him toward you, keep him on your left side and swing him to heel position. Use your left heel to straighten him out if he begins to sit behind you or crookedly. This may take a little work, but the dog will get the idea if you show him just what you want.

THE "STAND"

Your Shorthair should be trained to stand on one spot without moving his feet, and should allow a stranger to run his hands over his body and legs without showing any resentment or fear. Use the same method you used in training him to stay on the sit and down. While walking, place your left hand out, palm toward his nose, and command him to stay. His first impulse will be to sit, so be prepared to stop that by placing your hand under his body. If he's really stubborn, you may have to wrap the lead around his body near his hindquarters and hold him up until he gets the idea that this is different from the command to sit. Praise him for standing and walk to the end of the lead. Correct him strongly if he starts to move. Have a stranger approach him and run his hands over the dog's back and down his legs. Keep him standing until

Use the method of professional trainers to help your German Shorthair perfect the stand. Place your left hand under the dog's tail to encourage him to keep it erect, with your right hand under his nose.

you come back to him. Walk around him from his left side, come to heel position, and let the dog sit as you praise him lavishly.

RETRIEVING

It's fun to teach your dog to fetch things on command. Use a wooden dumbbell, a thick dowel stick or a thin, rolled-up magazine. While you have the dog heeling on lead, hold the object in front of him and tease him by waving it in front of his nose. Then say "Take it" and let him grab it. Walk with him while he's carrying it, and then say "Give" and take it from his mouth. If he drops it first, pick it up and tease him until he takes it again and holds it until you remove it.

With the dog still on lead, throw the object a few feet in front of him and encourage him to pick it up and hold it. If he won't give it up when you want it, don't have a tug-of-war. Just blow into his nostrils and he'll release his hold. Then praise him as if he had given it to you willingly.

Don't become discouraged if he seems slow in getting the idea of retrieving. Sometimes it takes several months before the dog will go after an object and bring it to you, but, with patience and persistence, he'll succeed.

Don't expect to accomplish all the training overnight. Generally a dog-training school will devote about 10 weeks, with one session a week, to all this training. Between lessons the dogs and their masters are expected to work about 15 minutes every day on the exercises.

If you'd like more detailed information on training your dog, you'll find it in the pages of HOW TO HOUSEBREAK AND TRAIN YOUR DOG.

Your easy-going, responsive Shorthair can be trained to jump obstacles rather easily. Notice the grace of this animal as he takes the hurdle. A loving pat from his master afterward will motivate the dog to repeat the feat, and to go on to even greater tests of obedience.

It's important to remember that your German Shorthair has the natural instincts of a hunter, but it's your responsibility to develop them. If you train him to associate gun shots with food, for example, later when he is in the field he will associate shots with the pleasant task of tracking down the game. Unless you are cautious about introducing your dog to shots, however, he may become gun-shy.

There are dog-training classes in all parts of the country, some sponsored by the local A.S.P.C.A. A free list of dog-training clubs and schools is available from the Gaines Dog Research Center, 250 Park Avenue, New York, New York.

If you feel that you lack the time or the skill to train your dog yourself, there are professional dog trainers who will do it for you, but basically dog training is a matter of training *you* and your dog to work together as a team, and if you don't do it yourself you will miss a lot of fun.

ADVANCED TRAINING AND OBEDIENCE TRIALS

Once you begin training your dog and see how well he does, you'll probably be bitten by the "obedience bug"—the desire to enter him in obedience trials held under American Kennel Club license. Most dog shows now include obedience classes at which your dog can qualify for his "degrees" to demonstrate his usefulness as a companion dog, not merely as a pet or show dog.

The A.K.C. obedience trials are divided into three classes: Novice, Open and Utility.

In the Novice Class, the dog will be judged on the following basis:

Test	Maximum Score
Heel on leash	35
Stand for examination by judge	30
Heel free—off leash	45
Recall (come on command)	30
1-minute sit (handler in ring)	30
3-minute down (handler in ring)	30
Maximum total score	200

If the dog "qualifies" in three different shows by earning at least 50 per cent of the points for each test, with a total of at least 170 for the trial, he has earned the Companion Dog degree and the letters C.D. are entered in the stud book after his name.

After the dog has qualified as a C.D., he is eligible to enter the Open Class competition where he will be judged on this basis:

Test	Maximum Score
Heel free	40
Drop on recall	30
Retrieve (wooden dumbbell) on flat	25
Retrieve over obstacle (hurdle)	35
Broad jump	20
3-minute sit (handler out of ring)	25
5-minute down (handler out of ring)	25
Maximum total score	200

Again he must qualify in three shows for the C.D.X. (Companion Dog Excellent) title and then is eligible for the Utility Class where he can earn the Utility Dog degree in these rugged tests:

The simplest test of obedience in the novice class is heeling on leash. Always hold the lead in your right hand and keep the dog on your left side. Start him off right—soon your dog will heel even when he is off the leash.

Test	Maximum Score
Scent discrimination (picking up article handled by master from group of articles)—Article 1	20
Scent discrimination—Article 2	20
Scent discrimination—Article 3	20
Seek back (picking up article dropped by handler)	30
Signal exercise (heeling, etc., on hand signal only)	35
Directed jumping (over hurdle and bar jump)	40
Group examination	35
	——
Maximum total score	200

For more complete information about these obedience trials, write to the American Kennel Club, 221 Park Avenue South, New York 3, N.Y., and ask for their free booklet "Regulations and Standards for Obedience Trials." Spayed females and dogs that are disqualified from breed shows because of physical defects (see the Standards in Chapter 1) are eligible to compete in these trials.

Field training begins with long walks in the field. When your Shorthaired Pointer is about three months old, you can let him roam woods and fields to get accustomed to their new sights and smells. At first, he will be excited and puppyish, but at the age of six or seven months, your dog will develop a more serious attitude toward game. Begin serious training when he shows signs of stalking.

Never use a wounded bird in training a working retriever. This dog has brought back a dead bird which has had its wings tied together. If possible, let your novice retriever work with an experienced dog. He will learn from observing the other dog's and chances are, he will become skilled much faster than if he had been trained alone.

Besides the formal A.K.C. obedience trials, there are informal "match" shows in which dogs compete for ribbons and inexpensive trophies. These shows are run by many local fanciers' dog clubs and by all-breed obedience clubs, and in many localities the A.S.P.C.A. and other groups conduct their own obedience shows. Your local pet shop or kennel can keep you informed about such shows in your vicinity and you will find them listed in the different dog magazines or in the pet column of your local paper, along with information on field trials.

FIELD TRAINING THE GERMAN SHORTHAIRED POINTER

While some Shorthairs have qualified both in formal obedience work and in the field, many experts think that the dog who is to be used for hunting should not be given the obedience training just described. They think that acquiring the obedience routines may stifle the natural "field" instincts of the dog.

The subject of field training has been covered in many books. Here we will just discuss it briefly.

When he is about three months of age you can take the Shorthair out for walks in the field and allow him to investigate the new sights and smells. Encourage him to flush out and chase birds and small field animals. Give him full freedom at this stage.

When he is about six or seven months old you will probably note a difference in his attitude toward the game he finds. He should begin to approach the birds in a more purposeful manner and his approach should become more of a stalk than puppyish abandon. At this stage, you can begin his training.

If he is reluctant to give you the bird, never try to force it out of your dog's mouth. Coax him in a gentle, affectionate voice. When he lets go, reward him with pats and compliments.

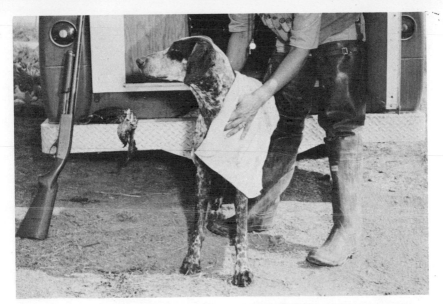

After a hard day of waterfowling, you will need a rest—and so will your Shorthair. Always show him that you appreciate his good performance.

THE TRAINING EQUIPMENT

For field training, you will need the following equipment:

1. Chain choke collar.
2. 25-foot check rope of sash cord.
3. Whistle.
4. Blank training pistol.

Most trainers prefer to carry on early training in the yard rather than in the field with its many distractions. The first step should be to teach the dog to "go" and to "come." Every time you turn the dog loose, give a sharp, short double blast on the whistle. In time he will associate this with the act of going away. The signal to come in is a lower, prolonged blast of the whistle, and here you can use the check rope to help him associate the signal with what you want him to do. At first you may have to use voice signals to supplement the whistle signal, but with patience your dog will get the idea.

The novice field dog must be trained to stop on command. Here, again, you can use the check rope to good advantage. When the dog is running free (preferably after a bird), shout "Whoa." It won't do any good, but just as he reaches the end of the check rope, give it a good yank, shouting "Whoa" again. After a couple of involuntary somersaults, he'll get the idea that it's a good thing to stop fast when he hears you holler "Whoa."

Once you have taught the dog these basics, take him out in the field and work close to him, teaching him to remain steady on a point. Some dog people claim that natural hunting dogs learn from observing one another in the field,

"Good show!" Whenever your dog is cooperative and performs well, praise him lavishly. Like people, dogs are best motivated by approval. In fact, when you disapprove of what he has done, it is often enough to simply *withhold* praise. Automatically, he will try to please you next time.

The versatile Shorthair is just as comfortable around the house as in the field. He is an easily trained watchdog and will quickly develop a protective attitude toward his family —even toward a family which includes a cat. He will be just as patient with tabby's smugness as with rough, but sincere, outbursts of affection from children.

Once trained, your Shorthaired Pointer will be a welcome companion on any trip. Because of his size, he doesn't take up too much space and can easily adapt to small quarters.

and working with an experienced dog and handler can help both you and your dog to acquire the finer points of field work.

Most Shorthairs take naturally to retrieving, but if yours hesitates, try using the technique described on page 43.

There is no reason why your dog should be gun-shy if he first hears a gunshot under the right circumstances. It is a good idea to fire a pistol some distance away just as the puppy comes out to his food dish. With a few repetitions, he will associate the sound of the shot with food. Gradually bring the shooting range closer, until he accepts a shot close by as a signal that something pleasant —food—is next on his schedule. Then it should be easy to get him to accept the gunshot as part of the pleasant enjoyment of seeking out game and retrieving it. Keep in mind that puppies invariably fear any loud, sudden unknown sounds and a wrong approach to gunfire may produce a gun-shy dog that will never be able to work in the field. Don't try to bring your puppy up to a firing line on the theory that subjecting him to a lot of gunfire may immunize him to the sound of a shot; it probably will have the opposite effect.

When you are training your Shorthair, remember that his ancestors have been hunting as long as yours, and that he has the natural instincts of the sporting dog; your part is to help him bring them out.

6. Caring for the Female and Raising Puppies

Whether or not you bought your female dog intending to breed her, some preparation is necessary when and if you decide to take this step.

WHEN TO BREED

It is usually best to breed in the second or third season. Plan in advance the time of year which is best for you, taking into account where the puppies will be born and raised. You will keep them until they are at least 6 weeks old, and a litter of frisky pups takes up considerable space by then. Other considerations are selling the puppies (Christmas vs. springtime sales), your own vacation, and time available to care for them. You'll need at least an hour a day to feed and clean up after the mother and puppies but probably it will take you much longer—with time out to admire and play with them!

CHOOSING THE STUD

You can plan to breed your female about 6½ months after the start of her last season, although a variation of a month or two either way is not unusual. Choose the stud dog and make arrangements well in advance. If you are breeding for show stock, which may command better prices, a mate should be chosen with an eye to complementing the deficiencies of your female. If possible, they should have several ancestors in common within the last two or three generations, as such combinations generally "click" best. He should have a good show record or be the sire of show winners if old enough to be proven.

The owner of such a male usually charges a fee for the use of the dog. The fee varies. This does not guarantee a litter, but you generally have the right to breed your female again if she does not have puppies. In some cases the owner of the stud will agree to take a choice puppy in place of a stud fee. You should settle all details beforehand, including the possibility of a single surviving puppy, deciding the age at which he is to make his choice and take the pup, and so on.

If you want to raise a litter "just for the fun of it" and plan merely to make use of an available male of the breed, the most important point is temperament. Make sure the dog is friendly as well as healthy, because a bad disposition could appear in his puppies, and this is the worst of all traits in a dog destined to be a pet. In such cases a "stud fee puppy," not necessarily the choice of the litter, is the usual payment.

If you decide to breed your female Shorthair, select a male whose positive qualities will complement any weaknesses she may have. He should be in first-rate physical condition, responsive and friendly by disposition.

The German Shorthaired Pointer Club of America, parent club of the breed, is a good source of information when you are looking for a mate for your dog. Many members have stud dogs available, and if you want to breed your female, it will be worth while to join the club. The American Kennel Club will give you, on request, the name and address of the Secretary of the Club.

PREPARATION FOR BREEDING

Before you breed your female, make sure she is in good health. She should be neither too thin nor too fat. Any skin disease *must* be cured, before it can be passed on to the puppies. If she has worms she should be wormed before being bred or within three weeks afterward. It is generally considered a good idea to revaccinate her against distemper and hepatitis before the puppies are born. This will increase the immunity the puppies receive during their early, most vulnerable period.

The female will probably be ready to breed 12 days after the first colored discharge. You can usually make arrangements to board her with the owner of the male for a few days, to insure her being there at the proper time, or you can take her to be mated and bring her home the same day. If she still appears receptive she may be bred again two days later. However, some females never show signs of willingness, so it helps to have the experience of a breeder. Usually the second day after the discharge changes color is the proper time, and she may be bred for about three days following. For an additional week or so she may have some discharge and attract other dogs by her odor, but can seldom be bred.

Keep your whelping female warm and comfortable. She will know what to do during birth, but it will be easier for her if she can see you nearby, ready to assist if necessary. Of course, if complications appear, she should have her puppies at the veterinarian's instead of at home.

THE FEMALE IN WHELP

You can expect the puppies 9 weeks from the day of breeding, although 61 days is as common as 63. During this time the female should receive normal care and exercise. If she was overweight, don't increase her food at first; excess weight at whelping time is bad. If she is on the thin side build her up, giving her a morning meal of cereal and egg yolk. You may add one of the mineral and vitamin supplements to her food, to make sure that the puppies will be healthy. As her appetite increases, feed her more. During the last weeks the puppies grow enormously and she will probably have little room for food and less appetite. She should be tempted with meat, liver and milk, however.

As the female in whelp grows heavier, cut out violent exercise and jumping. Although a dog used to such activities will often play with the children or run around voluntarily, restrain her for her own sake. However, don't eliminate exercise entirely. Walking is very beneficial to the female in whelp, and a daily moderate walk will help her keep up her "muscle tone" in preparation for the birth.

PREPARING FOR THE PUPPIES

Prepare a whelping box a few days before the puppies are due, and allow the mother to sleep there overnight or to spend some time in it during the day to become accustomed to it. Then she is less likely to try to have her pups under the front porch or in the middle of your bed. The box should have a wooden floor. Sides about a foot high will keep the puppies in but enable the mother to get out after she has fed them. If the weather is cold, the box should be raised about an inch off the floor.

Layers of newspaper spread over the whole area will make excellent bedding and be absorbent enough to keep the surface warm and dry. They should be removed daily and replaced with another thick layer. An old quilt or washable blanket makes better footing for the nursing puppies than slippery newspaper during the first week, and is softer for the mother.

Be prepared for the actual whelping several days in advance. Usually the female will tear up papers, refuse food and generally act restless. These may be false alarms; the real test is her temperature, which will drop to below 100° about 12 hours before whelping. Take it with a rectal thermometer morning and evening, and put her in the pen, looking in on her frequently, when the temperature goes down.

WHELPING

Usually little help is needed but it is wise to stay close to your pet to make sure that the mother's lack of experience does not cause an unnecessary accident. If anything seems wrong, waste no time in calling your veterinarian. You may want his experience in whelping the litter even if all goes well. He will probably prefer to have the puppies born at his hospital rather than to get up in the middle of the night to come to your home. The mother would, no doubt, rather stay at home, but you can be sure she will get the best of care in his hospital.

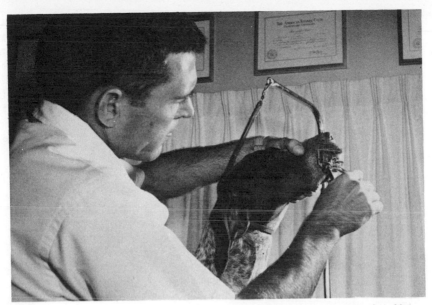

Above: If your dog seems to have championship qualities, you may want to show him. For this purpose a little special grooming is required. For example, you will want to have stray hairs removed from his jaw and neck.

Below: Your Shorthair's bobbed tail will need some sprucing up too if you are going to show him.

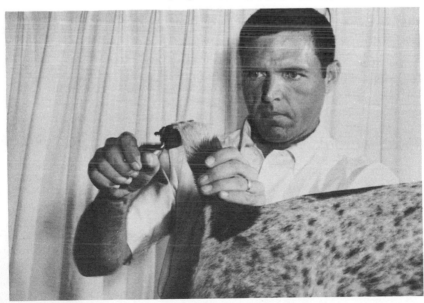

If the birth takes place at home, be ready to aid the mother when the first puppy arrives, for it could smother if she does not break the membrane enclosing it. She should start right away to lick the puppy, drying and stimulating it, but you can do it with a soft rough towel, instead. The afterbirth should follow the birth of each puppy, attached to the puppy by the long umbilical cord. Watch to make sure that each is expelled anyway, for retaining this material can cause infection. In her instinct for cleanliness the mother will probably eat the afterbirth after biting the cord. One or two will not hurt her; they stimulate milk supply as well as labor for remaining pups. But too many can make her lose appetite for the food she needs to feed her pups and regain her strength. So remove the rest of them along with the wet newspapers and keep the pen dry and clean to relieve her anxiety.

If the mother does not bite the cord, or does it too close to the body, take over the job, to prevent an umbilical hernia. Tearing is recommended, but you can cut it, about two inches from the body, with a sawing motion of scissors, sterilized in alcohol. Then dip the end in a shallow dish of iodine; the cord will dry up and fall off in a few days.

The puppies should follow each other at intervals of not more than half an hour. If more time goes past and you are sure there are still pups to come, a brisk walk outside may start labor again. If she is actively straining without producing a puppy it may be presented backward, a so-called "breech" or upside down birth. Careful assistance with a well-soaped finger to feel for the puppy or ease it back may help, but never attempt to pull it by force against the mother.

Prepare a warm place to put the puppies after they are born to keep them dry and help them to a good start in life. Cover an electric heating pad or hot-water bottle with flannel and put it in the bottom of a cardboard box. Set the box near the mother so that she can see her puppies. She will usually allow you to help, but don't take the puppies out of sight, and let her handle things if your interference seems to make her nervous.

RAISING THE PUPPIES

Hold each puppy to a breast as soon as he is dry, for a good meal without competition. Then he may join his littermates in the box, out of his mother's way while she is whelping. Keep a supply of evaporated milk on hand for emergencies, or later weaning. A formula of evaporated milk, corn syrup and a little water with egg yolk should be warmed and fed in a doll or baby bottle if necessary. A supplementary feeding often helps weak pups over the hump. Keep track of birth weights and take weekly readings so you will have an accurate record of the pups' growth and health.

After the puppies have arrived, take the mother outside for a walk and drink, and then leave her to take care of them. She will probably not want to stay away more than a minute or two for the first few weeks. Be sure to keep water available at all times, and feed her milk or broth frequently, as she needs liquids to produce milk. To encourage her to eat, offer her the foods she likes best, until she asks to be fed without your tempting her. She will soon develop a ravenous appetite and should have at least two large meals a day, with dry food available in addition.

Be sure that all the puppies are getting enough to eat. If the mother sits or stands, instead of lying still to nurse, the probable cause is scratching from the puppies' nails. You can remedy this by clipping them, as you do hers. Manicure scissors will do for these tiny claws.

Some breeders advise disposing of the smaller or weaker pups in a large litter, as the mother has trouble in handling more than six or seven. But you can help her out by preparing an extra puppy box or basket. Leave half the litter with the mother and the other half in a warm place, changing off at two-hour intervals at first. Later you may change them less frequently, leaving them all together except during the day. Try supplementary feeding, too; as soon as their eyes open, at about two weeks, they will lap from a dish, anyway.

The puppies should normally be completely weaned at five weeks, although you start to feed them at three weeks. They will find it easier to lap semi-solid food. At four weeks they will eat four meals a day, and soon do without their mother entirely. Start them on mixed dog food, or leave it with them in a dish for self-feeding. Don't leave water with them all the time; at this age they play with everything and they will use it as a wading pool. They can drink all they need if it is offered several times a day, after meals.

As the puppies grow up the mother will go into the pen only to nurse them, first sitting up and then standing. To dry her up completely, keep the mother away for longer periods; after a few days of part-time nursing she can stay away for longer periods, and then completely. The little milk left will be reabsorbed.

AIRING THE PUPPIES

The puppies may be put outside, unless it is too cold, as soon as their eyes are open, and will benefit from the sunlight and vitamins. A rubber mat or newspapers underneath will protect them from cold or damp.

You can expect the pups to need at least one worming before they are ready to go to new homes, so take a stool sample to your veterinarian before they are three weeks old. If one puppy has worms all should be wormed. Follow the veterinarian's advice, and this applies also to vaccination. If you plan to keep a pup you will want to vaccinate him at the earliest age possible, so his litter-mates should be done at the same time.

7. Showing Your Shorthair

You probably think that your own Shorthair is the best in the country and possibly in the world, but before you enter the highly competitive world of the show, get some unbiased expert opinions. Compare your dog against standards on pages 7-10. If a fanciers' club in your vicinity is holding a match show, enter your dog and see what the judges think of him. If he places in a few match shows, then you might begin seriously considering the big-time shows. Visit a few as a spectator first and make careful mental notes of what is required of the handlers and the dogs. Watch how the experienced handlers manage their dogs to bring out their best points. See how they use pieces of liver to "bait" the dogs and keep them alert in the ring. If experts think your dog has the qualities to make him a champion, you might want to hire a professional handler to show him.

HOW TO ENTER

If your dog is purebred and registered with the American Kennel Club—or eligible for registration—you may enter him in the appropriate show class for which his age, sex and previous show record qualify him. You will find coming shows listed in the different dog magazines. Write to the secretary of the show, asking for the "Premium List." When you receive the entry form, fill it in carefully and send it back with the required entry fee. Then, before the show, you'll receive your Exhibitor's Pass which will admit you and your dog to the show.

Here are the five official show classes:

Puppy Class: Open to dogs at least 6 months and not more than 12 months of age. Limited to dogs whelped in the United States and Canada.

Novice Class: Open to dogs 6 months of age or older that have never won a first prize at a show—wins in puppy class excepted. Limited to dogs whelped in the United States or Canada.

Bred by Exhibitor Class: Open to all dogs except champions 6 months of age or over who are exhibited by the same person or kennel who was the recognized breeder on the records of the American Kennel Club.

American-Bred Class: Open to dogs that are not champions, 6 months of age or over, whelped in the United States after a mating which took place in the United States.

Open Class: Open to dogs 6 months of age or over, with no exceptions. In addition there are local classes, "special classes" and brace entries.

For full information on the dog show rules, see *How to Show Your Own Dog,* by Virginia Tuck Nichols (T.F.H.).

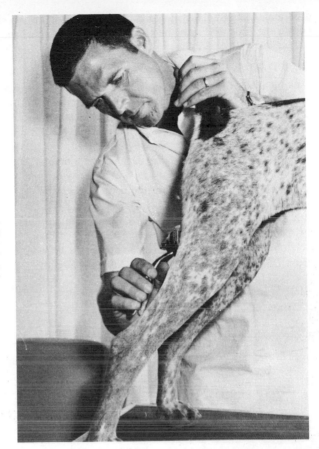

Uneven hairs should also be trimmed from a show dog's rear legs and hindquarters. The vet works carefully and, reassured by his expert touch, the dog is cooperative.

ADVANCE PREPARATION

Before you go to a show your dog should be trained to gait at a trot beside you, with head up and in a straight line. In the ring you will have to gait around the edge with other dogs and then individually up and down the center runner. In addition the dog must stand for examination by the judge, who will look at him closely and feel his head and body structure. He should be taught to stand squarely, hind feet slightly back, head up on the alert. He must hold the pose when you place his feet and show animation for a piece of boiled liver in your hand or a toy mouse thrown in front of you.

Showing requires practice training sessions in advance. Get a friend to act as judge and set the dog up and "show" him for a few minutes every day.

The day before the show, pack your kit. You will want to take a water dish and bottle of water for your dog (so that he won't be affected by a change in drinking water, and you won't have to go look for it). Take the show lead, the grooming tools and the identification ticket sent by the show superintendent, noting the time you must be there and the place where the show will be held, as well as the time of judging.

THE DAY OF THE SHOW

Don't feed your dog the morning of the show, or give him at most a light meal. He will be more comfortable in the car on the way, and will show more enthusiastically. When you arrive at the show grounds an official veterinarian will check your dog for health, and then you should find his bench and settle him there. Locate the ring where your breed will be judged, take the dog to the exercise ring to relieve himself, and give him a small drink of water. After a final grooming, you have only to wait until your class is called. It is your responsibility to be at the ring at the proper time.

Then, as you step into the ring, try to keep your knees from rattling too loudly. Before you realize it you'll be out again, perhaps back with the winners for more judging and finally—with luck—it will be all over and you'll have a ribbon and an armful of silver trophies. And a very wonderful dog!